FIRE ENGINES
IN COLOUR

S. W. STEVENS-STRATTEN

IAN ALLAN
Publishing

First published 1996

ISBN 0 7110 2332 8

© Ian Allan Ltd 1996

Published by Ian Allan Publishing

an imprint of Ian Allan Ltd, Terminal House, Station Approach, Shepperton, Surrey TW17 8AS.
Printed by Ian Allan Printing Ltd, Coombelands House, Coombelands Lane, Addlestone, Surrey KT15 1HY.

Introduction

Small boys get enthusiastic and excited when they see a fire engine. No matter whether it is rushing to an incident with blue lights flashing and sirens sounding, or whether it is stationary, it is always a point of great interest. I think this interest remains with most people all their lives.

The fire engine always seems to command attention, for there is a certain aura about this important vehicle.

Although this book is called Fire Engines in Colour, the word 'engine' is anathema in Fire Brigade circles, for it is always called an 'appliance' or a 'tender' where the latter name is appropriate.

This book is not intended to be a history of the fire service, although the contents are in chronological order and it is easy to see the vast changes that have been made over the years. It was not until the late 1930s that the enclosed or covered appliance made its appearance, as before this the fireman stood, or sat, on the open sides of the machine, known as the Braidwood body, named after a famous fire chief of the London Fire Brigade. It is doubtful whether the Health and Safety Act would allow such a position today, for apart from the fireman being exposed to inclement weather conditions, there was always the danger of him falling off — seat-belts were unheard of in those days — and should there have been an accident, there was a far greater likelihood of serious injury.

There have also been great changes in the equipment carried; for example, breathing apparatus is now a necessity, and the wheeled escape is now an item of the past as hydraulic platforms and snorkels have taken their place. The ladders themselves are now made of lightweight aluminium instead of the heavy wood, which of course was always likely to get burnt. The nature of calls (or 'shouts', as they are called) has changed and Brigades now face many different hazards, such as chemical incidents, hazardous materials, and of course rescue of victims trapped in road traffic accidents. They still rescue the odd cat stuck up a tree, but with the advent of central heating, chimney fires are less common.

The colour of fire appliances has also changed, and while red is still the predominant colour, yellow has been tried, and a large number of machines now have stainless steel panels. Chrome has replaced the old brass fittings. Likewise, with the exception of Dennis, the old manufacturers have closed down, and today there are several continental makes in Fire Brigade service.

There are of course variations in equipment and in technical specifications, which can be dictated by the Chief Fire Officer, or the appropriate committee of a Local Authority. Some may prefer a different make of pump, others may decide on a different layout of equipment.

We must not forget the debt of gratitude owed to the dedicated enthusiasts who have preserved the older appliances, often under extreme difficulties, for they are also preserving part of our heritage. Furthermore, without help we would be unable to produce this book in colour, for colour photography as we know it today, was only really established in the 1950s.

S. W. Stevens-Stratten
Epsom, Surrey
October 1995

Front Cover:
Austin pump escape unit. *Peter Durham*

Back Cover:
Dennis F12 fire appliance now in the service of a commercial organisation.
Peter Durham

Left:
The early fire pumps were manual ones and this Newsham of c1730 was operated by eight firemen (four each side) pulling the handles up and down. It has leather bellows, hose and buckets. It started life with the Holton Village Brigade in Oxfordshire, later passing to Wheatley Sawmills, where it was used for fire cover but also for pumping water into the Sawmills steam engine. The remains of this pump were discovered in 1967 when the Sawmills were cleared. It was sent to a scrap yard from where it was discovered and rebuilt by Mr Ned Passy. *K. Marshall*

Above left:
A Sarah Dickson Hose-cart of c1830. This cart was pulled by one or two firemen, and carried extra hose for the manual pump as well as extra buckets, axes, etc. It could possibly have carried such items as water bombs. Note the fireman in his traditional uniform. *K. Marshall*

Above right:
A small one-man-operated hand pump on the same principle as the larger model. This is the 'County' pump. *K. Marshall*

Left:
A horse-drawn Shand Mason steam-operated fire pump of 1908. This machine is typical of the period and was supplied to Lord Shaftesbury for his house at Wimborne St Giles, Dorset. It has now been faithfully preserved. The appliance weighs approx 35cwt unladen. *Bob Green*

Above:
A rear view of the same machine showing the boiler and pumps. The fire for the boiler was fanned by the passage of air as it went along the streets and by the time it arrived at the fire there was usually a good head of steam at 120lb pressure. The pumps could deliver 200–300 gallons per minute. *K. Marshall*

Far left:
One of the early motorised appliances; a 1912 Belsize pump escape supplied to Southampton City Council. Belsize was a Manchester firm established in 1906, who fitted this appliance with a 14.5 litre petrol engine developing 50/80hp, and Mather & Platt turbo pump giving 500 gallons per minute, and a 50ft John Morris wheeled escape. It was sold for an industrial works brigade in the 1950s. In 1961 it was purchased by the Enfield & District Veteran Vehicle Society for £50 in 1961.
Steve Greenaway

Left:
Dennis Bros of Guildford produced their first motorised fire engine in 1908. This example is a 1914 Dennis N type, supplied to the City of Coventry and had served for 20 years when sold to General Electric for their works brigade. The original solid tyres were changed to pneumatics and electric lighting installed. The machine remained in service until 1958 when it was purchased by Dennis Bros who have now preserved the machine. It has a White & Poppe nine-litre four-cylinder 60hp petrol engine.
Roger Pennington

Above:
Another Dennis N type which is still on solid tyres. This 1916 appliance was used by the London Fire Brigade for 20 years before it was sold to a Warrington soap works who used it until 1955. It is now in the custody of the Royal College of Science Motor Club. *Roger Pennington*

Above:
This 1923 model T Ford was built for Edward, Earl of Derby for his estate at Knowsley Hall. It is seen here
at the Yeovil Festival of Transport in August 1991. *Peter Durham*

Above:
Purchased in 1934 by the Avon India Rubber Co Ltd for use in their works at Melksham, Wiltshire. It is on a Dennis 30cwt chassis with a White & Poppe four-cylinder engine and is fitted with a 30ft wooden ladder and a Dennis No 2 pump. The purchase price was £667 5s, but it was sold at an auction in 1986 for £8.50. *Steve Greenaway*

Above:
Morris Commercial produced a few fire appliances in the 1930s. This is a 1934 model fitted with a 25hp 3486cc petrol engine and supplied new to the City of Worcester Police and Fire Brigade at a cost of £547 15s. The bodywork is by

B. S. Drewer. During the Blitz in World War 2 it was seconded to Coventry. In 1948 the Brigade workshops modified the body and fitted a rear-mounted Dennis pump. It was decommissioned in 1957 and restored in 1986.
Peter Durham

Above:
A Semi-forward control Morris Commercial model CS11/40F two-ton chassis with a six-cylinder 25hp
engine was supplied to Ind Coope, the Burton brewers in 1934. It is seen here at a rally at Duxford in 1979.
Steve Greenaway

Right:
Introduced in 1935, a popular machine was the Dennis 'Big Four' with a 30hp four-cylinder petrol engine and a Dennis No 3 two-stage turbine pump capable of issuing 500–700 gallons per minute. The pump could be side-mounted if required, but most were built with the pump at the rear. A 50ft Bailey wheeled escape is fitted. Supplied to Bedford Fire Service.
K. Marshall

Above:
A year later Dennis produced the 'Light Six' having the same wheelbase of 12ft 6in as the 'Big Four'. This time it had a 37hp six-cylinder petrol engine. Supplied new to Crowborough it remained in service with the East Sussex Fire Brigade until 1961 when it went to J. Lyons for their works brigade. It is now restored and preserved by a group of London firemen and seen at the HCVS London–Brighton run in 1995.
Peter Durham

Above:
A Leyland Cub FK6 pump escape which was new to Taunton in 1936, fitted with a six-cylinder engine developing 62bhp. The FK7 model was exactly the same except the pump was mounted at the side and either Rees-Rototurbo or Gwynne could be specified. *Steve Greenaway*

Above:
In 1933 Dennis produced their Ace chassis, known as the 'Pig' because of its protruding bonnet. It proved popular for fire service use; both the conventional Braidwood body and the 'New World' as shown here — where the firemen sat safely inside the body (exiting via the rear) and were thus not liable to be thrown off if the driver took a corner a little too fast! The Ace had a short wheelbase of only 9ft 6in and was fitted with 24hp engine. Supplied to Newhaven Fire Brigade, later retained by the East Sussex Fire Brigade until 1965 and now preserved. *J. Cawley*

Above:
An early example of the enclosed or limousine-type saloon body, fitted to a Dennis Ace with a Markham pump and used by the Sonning Fire Brigade.
Steve Greenaway

Above:
In 1937 Leyland produced the Lynx as a successor to their Cub chassis. This appliance was new to Skegness Urban District Council in 1937 as a hose reel/escape, but a year later a Dennis No 2 pump was fitted. It served with the Auxiliary Fire Service and National Fire Service and was later absorbed in the service of Lyndsey County Fire Service. Preserved in 1990 it has been refitted and signwritten to the original specification. *Steve Greenaway*

Left:
A 1939 Leyland Cub FK8 pump escape seen in a maroon and red colour scheme. The vehicle was supplied new to Loughborough in 1939.
Steve Greenaway

Right:
Several enclosed bodies were built on Leyland FK9 chassis as was this example supplied to Hinckley (Leics) in 1939. When it became the Leicestershire & Rutland Fire Service the livery was changed to a maroon and red colour scheme.
Steve Greenaway

Right:
New to Dartford Borough
Fire Brigade in 1939, this
Leyland FT4a pump
escape was in service until
1956 when it became a
training vehicle until 1971.
The 'Blued' metal bonnet
in lieu of ordinary paint is
to combat engine heat
which could discolour
paintwork. It was restored
in the workshops of the
Kent Fire Brigade and is
seen here at the end of the
HCVS London–Brighton
run in 1993.
Peter Durham

Above:
This 1938 Dennis 'Light Four' is unusual in that it has an enclosed cab for two (driver and senior fireman) while the other two crew members sit in the open on a Braidwood style body. Only a handful of this type were built with a Dennis 25hp four-cylinder side valve engine with an option of a four or five-speed gearbox.

A Dennis No 2 turbine pump was mounted at the rear. This appliance was new to the Leicestershire & Rutland Fire Brigade. Seen here at the Dennis 100th Anniversary Celebrations at Wroughton Airfield in July 1995.
Roger Pennington

Above:
New to Budleigh Salterton in 1939, this Leyland Cub FK8 served the town until 1947. During the Blitz it was sent to help at Bristol and Plymouth. It was transferred to Exmouth and last saw active service in Brixham. It was found derelict in 1987 and faithfully restored as seen at the Langport Steam Rally in July 1991. *Peter Durham*

Above:
Letchworth Garden City Fire Brigade chose a dark green for their livery which was applied to this 1934 Dennis 'Big Four' machine. It has seating for 10 men, a Dennis No 3 main pump and a 50ft Merryweather wheeled escape. It served with the Hertfordshire Brigade until 1963. *Steve Greenaway*

Above:
In the late 1930s several brigades ordered Leyland TLM turntable ladders. Built on a chassis based on the Tiger bus chassis, with a wheelbase of 14ft 6in, it was powered by a Leyland six-cylinder overhead valve petrol engine of 43.5hp, or there was an option of an engine with a larger bore which developed 49.8hp. The machines were all equipped with a 100ft Metz turntable ladder and normally had a Rees-Rototurbo 500 gallon per minute pump. This particular appliance has a five-section 104ft ladder and spent its life working with Macclesfield until sold in 1971. It has now been preserved.
S. W. Stevens-Stratten

Above:
With war clouds looming in 1938, the Home Office ordered some emergency fire appliances. They chose the Ford 7V chassis which had a V8 side valve petrol engine of 3622cc, 30hp. There were variations in the pumping equipment, usually a Tangye 700 gallon per minute unit. Some machines carried an escape, in which case an extended tow bar had to be provided for a trailer pump. Other variations had a front-mounted pump above the bumper. The extended cab roof gave the crew some protection from falling debris and shrapnel. All these vehicles were painted grey for the Auxiliary Fire Service (AFS) and later the National Fire Service (NFS).

This preserved example was seen at a fire brigade rally at Hickstead (Sussex) in 1994. *Steve Greenaway*

Above:
When the war started, many of the trailer pumps were towed by commandeered London taxis, which, although they did a valiant job, were not really suitable, especially for the larger and heavier pumps. Therefore the Home Office ordered large numbers of the Austin K2 (2-ton) chassis with a van type body for six men, hoses and other emergency equipment, with a 30ft ladder on the roof. *Steve Greenaway*

Above:
One of the wartime problems was water shortage, and to overcome this the mobile dam was created for the Auxiliary Fire Service. This is a Dodge model 82 designed for a 3–4 ton payload. It has a 13ft 6in wheelbase and was fitted with a Dodge six-cylinder petrol engine of 27.3hp. It has a Wynn pump driven from the power take off. *Steve Greenaway*

Above:
Similar duties to those of the Ford 7V were given to this Austin K4 wartime pump escape unit, but this view shows the front-mounted Barton pump which is driven from the vehicle's power take off.
Steve Greenaway

Above:
In addition to the Austin ATV, Ford were also requested to produce a similar vehicle. They used their WOT 2 chassis as used for the Army which the military rated as 15cwt. It had a 30hp V8 engine. This preserved example is seen at a rally at Duxford in May 1991. *Steve Greenaway*

Above:
A wartime shortage of turntable ladders led to the introduction of an Austin K4 chassis being used for a 60ft Merryweather of three sections which was manually operated. The unit was powered by a six-cylinder petrol engine of 3.5 litres. *Steve Greenaway*

Above:
Believed to be the only type of fire engine with a half-cab, these wartime turntable ladders were built on a Leyland Titan TD7 bus chassis. The 100ft ladder and fire equipment were supplied by Merryweather. This particular example of the few that were built, was allocated to the National Fire Service at Aberdeen, later passing to the North West Fire Service where it remained until 1966. *Steve Greenaway*

Above:
After the war, in 1948 the National Fire Service was disbanded and control handed back to local authorities and county councils.

Many retained the wartime appliances but repainted them from the drab grey to the conventional red. This gave them an entirely different appearance as seen here with a Leyland TD7/Merryweather turntable ladder which served Wolverhampton Fire Brigade. *Steve Greenaway*

Above:
A smart looking Austin Auxiliary Towing Vehicle in peacetime dress as it completes an HCVS
London–Brighton run in May 1990. *T. A. Brown*

Above:
A wartime Austin pump escape unit with front-mounted Barton pump which was retained in peacetime
by the Pembrokeshire Fire Brigade and is now preserved. *Steve Greenaway*

Above:
The last of the 'open' appliances to be built by Dennis was the F2 in 1949. Powered by a Rolls-Royce B80 engine, some were fitted with wheeled escapes, while others merely carried ladders. A large number of these machines were exported, but this example was new to the British Thompson Houston Co at their Rugby Works and served until 1977 when it went into private ownership. *Steve Greenaway*

Above:
In 1950 Dennis introduced their F12 model which was ordered in large numbers by authorities in the British Isles. Powered by the Rolls-Royce B80 straight eight-cylinder petrol engine which developed 160bhp, it had vacuum servo-assisted hydraulic brakes on all wheels, and a wheelbase of 12ft 6in. The model remained in production for nine years. This pump escape saw service with the Hampshire Fire Brigade and is now beautifully preserved.
Steve Greenaway

Above:
The offside view of a Dennis F12 appliance with the lockers open showing the equipment carried.
S. W. Stevens-Stratten

Above:
Several brigades used the Leyland Comet chassis, and Surrey Fire Brigade purchased six in 1952. This pump appliance was in service until 1966 when it was sold to Schermukly Ltd, firework manufacturers who used it until 1978. It was found derelict in the New Forest in 1985 and is now restored to its original condition. *Steve Greenaway*

Left:
About the same time, other brigades were purchasing Commer chassis with several different body manufacturers. This 1952 water tender has an HCB body and a Dennis pump capable of delivering 500 gallons per minute. It was new to the Kent Fire Brigade. *K. Marshall*

Above:
Apart from actual fire appliances, brigades also have emergency tenders carrying items not normally carried on the regular machines. This AEC Regent chassis has a Merryweather body and is now preserved in its original condition. *Steve Greenaway*

Right:
After the demise of the National Fire Service the Home Office set up the Auxiliary Fire Service again and ordered large numbers of Bedford S and R types, which could be used for any major national emergency. They became known as 'Green Goddesses' and were built between 1953–6, the earlier models being normal two-wheel drive, while the later ones were all four-wheel drive. Powered by a Bedford six-cylinder petrol engine of 110bhp (4927cc), they carry a 400-gallon water tank, a Sigmund 5,900 gallon per minute pump, a light portable pump and a 35ft metal ladder. All were painted green, but some were later purchased by brigades and put into red livery. The example shown here is sucking water from waterlogged parts of Chichester following the floods of 1993. The tarpaulin at the rear is to protect the crew from further rain.
Nigel Tipping

Above:
The Green Goddesses were also to form a mobile column of vehicles which could move quickly to any part of the country. To enable water to be taken from lakes or rivers, a vehicle carrying three inflatable rafts and nine portable pumps was provided. These were mounted on a Commer Q4 4x4 chassis, and were known as 'Bikini Units'. *Steve Greenaway*

Above:
A 1953 Ford Thames/Firefly water pump/foam tender was supplied to some Royal Ordnance factories and county brigades. The chassis is the standard Ford product. The example shown here has been restored and is now preserved. *Steve Greenaway.*

Above:
The Dennis F8 model is very similar to the F12, but has a shorter wheelbase (10ft) and has the Rolls-Royce
B60 six-cylinder engine giving 175bhp. It carries a 300-gallon first aid tank. *Steve Greenaway*

Above:
Another version of a Dennis F8, but with Miles bodywork, which was new in 1955. *Steve Greenaway*

Right:
A 1956 Bedford S type chassis which was popular with many brigades during the 1950s. A variety of different body styles were developed by several manufacturers. This example was originally with the Suffolk Fire Service but was later sold to the Aylesbury Health Authority and stationed at Stone Hospital. *Peter Durham*

Above:
Around the early 1950s AEC produced some fire engine chassis. This AEC Mercury with a 7.5-litre diesel engine has Merryweather Marquis fire equipment. The wheelbase is 13ft 6in. The pump can deliver 950 gallons per minute at 70lb pressure. Two 180ft hose reels can be fed from the 100-gallon first aid tank. It is typical of the type. *Peter Durham*

Above:
The first diesel-engined fire appliance from Dennis was the model F101 in 1956. Normally a Rolls-Royce engine was fitted, but there was an option for a Perkins engine. They had a four-speed crash gearbox and a Dennis No 3 1,000 gallons per minute pump. A Bayley 50ft wheeled wooden escape was fitted as well as hook and scaling ladders. Two sets of breathing apparatus were also carried. The F101 model was supplied to London with single rear tyres, but other authorities specified twins at the rear. *S. W. Stevens-Stratten*

Left:
A 1957 Bedford S type water tower which has now been preserved and is seen at the Sandwell Historic Vehicle Rally in May 1987. *D. Badger*

Above:
In 1958 the London Fire Brigade took delivery of this Dennis F103 emergency tender. It was powered by a Dennis 120bhp six-cylinder diesel engine. Fully loaded it was capable of 55mph on level ground. The overall length was 27ft 6in. Very few were built. *Steve Greenaway*

Above:
Some brigades who served country areas found that a small appliance had advantages when negotiating narrow lanes etc. This 1958 Austin Gypsy with its 2000cc engine was originally based at St Mawes in Cornwall. It is now preserved and fully equipped and in working order. *Peter Durham*

Above:
A front view of an Austin Gypsy showing the front-mounted pump. *Roger Pennington*

Left:
The Dennis F24 and F28 models were very similar except that the F28 was only 7ft 6in wide. *Roger Pennington*

Above:
This Hampshire Car Bodies (HCB) bodywork on a Bedford S type chassis was a pump escape supplied in 1960 to the Isle of Wight Fire Service. *Steve Greenaway*

Above:
Only 10 examples of the Leyland Firemaster were ever built; two of them being turntable ladders as illustrated here. A horizontal 9.8-litre Leyland diesel engine, giving 150bhp, was mounted amidships, with a four-speed semi-automatic epicyclic gearbox, and a 500 gallon per minute Coventry Climax pump was located at the front. A 100ft hydraulic Magirus ladder was fitted but later changed to Carmichael equipment. *Steve Greenaway*

Above:
A 1963 Karrier Gamecock, which is virtually the same as the Commer, and is seen in many fire services. *T. A. Brown*

Above:
A Bedford J2 appliance with HCB bodywork as supplied to the Devon Fire Service in 1964 and stationed at Lynton, where it was ideal for narrow streets and steep hills. *Peter Durham*

Above:
In the 1960s, AEC in conjunction with Merryweather produced several turntable ladders, as seen in this example with a 100ft ladder supplied to Blackburn Fire Brigade and now in preservation. *Steve Greenaway*

Above:
A later example, from 1967, of a Merryweather turntable ladder on an AEC chassis, but this time with the later ergonomic tilt cab. This was supplied to Cardiff City Fire Brigade. *Steve Greenaway*

Right:
In 1966 Dennis supplied this attractive model F107 emergency unit to the Cardiff City Fire Service.
Eric H. Sawford

Above:
ERF entered the field of fire appliance manufacturers briefly in the late 1960s. The bodywork was by an associated company, J. H. Jennings & Son Ltd. They all had the distinctive cab and were fitted with a 170hp Perkins V8 diesel engine, while most had David Brown gearboxes. They ceased manufacture of fire appliances in 1981. This machine was supplied to the Cardiff City Fire Service in 1970. *Steve Greenaway*

Right:
Some ERFs were built as turntable ladders or with hydraulic platforms. This machine was supplied to Manchester Fire Brigade in 1974 and carried a 50ft TSM Simonitor, a cross between a hydraulic platform and a pump escape. It was sold in the mid-1980s.
Simon Rowley

Above:
Some fire appliances used the Land Rover chassis as it was ideal for working in confined conditions in the country. This 1967 MkII Land Rover has Merryweather equipment and was supplied to the Central Electricity Generating Board at their Pembroke Power Station. It is seen here on its first day after restoration at the Stonehouse Rally in Gloucestershire in September 1992. *Peter Durham*

Above:
Some brigades ordered the forward control Land Rover as seen in this example from the Isle of Man.
Steve Greenaway

Above:
This 1970 Dennis D type is typical of the period. This water tender has a first aid tank of either 100 or 400 gallons. It was also offered with a Jaguar 4.2 litre six-cylinder petrol engine (on early models), or a Rolls-Royce B61 petrol engine, or a Perkins diesel engine. It had a Dennis No 2 pump capable of delivering 500 gallons per minute. Many were used by the London Fire Brigade, but this example was supplied to the Southampton Fire Brigade. *Steve Greenaway*

Above:
Dodge entered the fire appliance market in the 1970s; their chassis being bodied by various coachbuilders and with different makes of equipment.

The engine was often a Perkins V8 diesel of 180bhp. This machine was delivered to the Fife Fire & Rescue Service in 1977. *Ken Reid*

Above:
Two years later Fife Fire & Rescue took delivery of another Dodge, with different bodywork and appearance from the previous appliance. *Ken Reid*

Above:
An Ogle designed cab was fitted to the Shelvoke make when they entered the market in the 1980s. Their production of appliances was short-lived, although they supplied both London and Surrey brigades among others. This was a Strathclyde Fire Brigade pump/water tender new in 1983. *Ken Reid*

Left:
Hertfordshire County Council operate this 1987 Dennis Snorkel hydraulic platform, which is stationed at Watford. It is seen here at the Dennis Centenary Celebrations at Wroughton Airfield in May 1995. *Roger Pennington*

Above:
A 1989 Volvo FL6 chassis with Alexander bodywork — this latter firm being generally noted for its bus coachwork — in the service of Fife Fire & Rescue. Note the 'bar' type blue flashing light unit, which now often replaces the two flashers. *Ken Reid*

Above:
In the same year the Lothian and Borders Fire Brigade took delivery of a Renault appliance. At that time very few of this make were evident in the British Isles. *Ken Reid*

Right:
Demountable bodies have now become commonplace for breathing apparatus, hose reel layers, salvage units, and even command control vehicles. The idea is that the brigade need only a few bare chassis at strategic locations, and whichever body is required the chassis merely backs on to the raised unit and it is on its way. This 1990 Scania is a normal truck chassis used by the Grampian Fire Brigade. *Ken Reid*

Above:
This 1993 Volvo has a crew compartment which is separate from the driver's cab. It is operated by the Tayside Fire Brigade. *Ken Reid*

Above:
The latest from Dennis is the Rapier, as shown in this 1994 appliance operated by the Wiltshire Fire Service, which is being put through its paces at the Dennis Centenary Celebrations. The special chassis gives a lower floor-line than conventional machines, thus giving easier access for the crew and to the equipment. It also has greater stability on the road, with independent front suspension. It is fitted with a Cummins 250bhp C-series 8.2 litre diesel engine (others from this range can be specified). It also has automatic transmission, and special ABS anti-locking braking system, which ensures straight line braking from speeds of up to 75mph. *Roger Pennington*

Above:
The canteen van is a welcome sight at a major conflagration and a variety of vehicles are used, often a conversion of a normal commercial vehicle. This 1972 Bedford TK serves crews in the Hampshire Fire Brigade. *Steve Greenaway*

Above:

Airport fire crews are specially trained to deal with aircraft crashes and subsequent fires. The ability to deliver gallons of foam quickly and to run 'off-the-road' are prime requisites of an airport fire appliance. This 1972 Thornycroft 6x6 (actually manufactured by Scammell) has Carmichael equipment. Note the foam tanks and the foam nozzle which can be directed through 360°. *R. Matthews*

Above:
An older Thornycroft 6x6, but still capable of giving valuable service. This appliance is fitted with Pyrene equipment. *Steve Greenaway*

Above:
A modern Scania, which has Simon equipment, is one of the appliances at Belfast Airport, and is more of a conventional machine with a small foam nozzle fixed to the front bumper. *Ken Reid*

The 'Heyday' series from IAN ALLAN
Publishing

The Heyday of the Classic Bus (reprint)
By Gavin Booth   ISBN: 0711022275   7.5in x 9.5in   Paper over board
£11.99

The Heyday of the Classic Coach
By Kevin Lane   ISBN: 0711022704   7.5in x 9.5in   Paper over board
£11.99

The Heyday of the European Tram
By Peter Waller   ISBN: 0711022747   7.5in x 9.5in   Paper over board
£10.99

The Heyday of London's Buses
By Kevin McCormack   ISBN: 071102121X   7.5in x 9.5in   Paper over board
£10.99

The Heyday of London's Buses - 2
By Kevin McCormack   ISBN: 0711023441   7.5in x 9.5in   Paper over board
£10.99

The Heyday of the Trolleybus
By Howard Piltz   ISBN: 0711022712   7.5in x 9.5in   Paper over board
£11.99

The Heyday of the British Lorry
By Malcolm Broad (text), Peter Durham (photographs)   ISBN: 0711023867
7.5in x 9.5in   Paper over board   **£10.99**

The Heyday of the Traction Engine
By Eric Sawford   ISBN: 071102362X   7.5in x 9.5in   Paper over board   **£10.99**